Playing with Poetry

Playing with Poetry: A handbook making poetry playful and inspiring
© Jude Comerford, Sue Elmes, Dianna Fames, and Kate Kennedy 2023

All rights reserved. No part of this publication may be reproduced, stored in a retrieval system, or transmitted in any form or by any means, electronic, mechanical, photocopying, recording or otherwise, without the prior written permission of the authors.

ISBN: 978-1-922784-81-0 (Paperback)

Cover Image: Kent Lyons and Sue Elmes
Images in use: Sue Elmes
Cover Design: Clark & Mackay
Design and Typeset: Clark & Mackay
Printed in Australia by Clark & Mackay

Published by Jude Comerford, Sue Elmes, Dianna Fames, and Kate Kennedy with assistance by Clark & Mackay

www.clark-mackay.com.au

Contents

Welcome Chat from the Authors..1
Why Take This Journey?..3
How to Use This Handbook 6
Let's Begin 7
Topic 1: Gardens..11
Topic 2: Childhood Memories..25
Topic 3: Obsession..39
Topic 4: Illnesses and Personal Crisis 53
Topic 5: Shakespeare..71
Topic 6: Meditation for Creativity 87
Author's Concluding Chats 101
Topic: Just for Enjoyment and Inspiration..105

About the Authors..127
Bibliography 131

Welcome Chat from the Authors

When we started this group, we had no idea we were going to write a book. The joy of sharing our writing was so nourishing that we felt we had to share our thoughts and ideas with others who might be struggling or needing a pickup.

We missed our friends and found a way to lift our spirits. Isolation was dragging us down, and we found that we had something important to say.

In challenging times, we must give ourselves a break, ease up on the demands we put on ourselves and accept credit for doing our best.

We are a group of four middle-aged women of European heritage influenced predominantly by Australian and European literary ideas. However, the world is a beautiful, diverse and interesting place, and all cultures have their own unique literary and artistic heritage.

We would encourage you to move outside your literary comfort zone and embrace and explore works from other cultures. In this age of the internet, this is easier to do than ever before.

Why Take This Journey?

Have you ever been curious about whether you could write poetry or even have fun doing it? Writing poetry can be a celebration of something or someone, or a way to dump those unwanted thoughts that keep haunting you.

Here is an example of how writing poetry has helped and inspired some of our authors.

"I have always written. In times of stress and serious illness, I have found that writing, especially in poetry form, was helpful. The act of writing helps me download my deepest worries and fears and has allowed me to let go, or at least come to terms with them. Poetry is tight and concise and lets me get to the nitty gritty of my distress without having to expend too much energy. I also love the fact that I can sometimes capture moments of beauty and emotion. These are not always poems I share, especially with family members, but some will be part of the legacy I leave to my children."

—Sue Elmes

"I was driving in the late afternoon with a storm coming on and was suddenly surrounded by a corridor of jacaranda blossoms. It slowed me down as I drove across the carpet. The backdrop of the jacarandas was intensified by a storm brewing. I felt myself letting go of all my stress and entering a state of calm. It blew my mind, and I didn't know how to express it. Words came to me and I couldn't wait to get home to write it down. Suddenly it was a poem. And no one was more surprised than me."

—Jude Comerford

"Writing poetry calms me no matter what the topic. As I concentrate on writing, it takes my mind away from all that is worrying me. I often write a poem to friends or family to express how I feel about them. Sometimes I frame it or put it into a birthday card."

—Kate Kennedy

"Writing sets the matter apart from you. You can see the matter more clearly. It has distance from you. You can make out its shape and substance. You can begin to reason with something that has dimensions and components. You can then choose to embrace it, or discard it or just sit with it. Whatever matters to you."

—Dianna Fames

So, you see poetry can be used for many reasons. You choose what you write about and how you want to write it.

Here's the Good News

You don't need any previous writing ability.
    You don't have to think of yourself as artistic.
    Writing poetry can be quickly achieved using simple ideas.

Your creative juices can bubble up even when you didn't know you had any.

You can write just for yourself or start a group, as the authors did, with some like-minded supportive friends.

Here's the Bad News

Well, there isn't any bad news! Just go for it and enjoy.

Words of Wisdom

Don't get caught up in what other people think. If the final product expresses how you feel and gives you a sense of satisfaction, then you are a poet. It is the process that rewards, and the poem is a bonus.

Poetry has many different forms. Some forms include rhyme. Some have a set number of lines like a sonnet. Some people make their own rules. Poetry can be very structured and formal or free flowing and loose. The important learning for our group was that we, as individuals, decided on a starting point and then just wrote. If you let go of your internal critic, this will work for you too. So, let's get writing.

How to Use This Handbook

First and foremost, the handbook is designed to be flexible.
There is a series of topics. Each topic contains:
- Poems by the authors.
- Activities that prompt the writing of your own poem.

It's your choice. You can start:
- At the beginning and work through it systematically.
- Choose a topic that takes your interest.
- Or work alone or with a friend.

It's up to you.

If you would like to work with a group of people with similar interests, a small group is more effective, supportive and enjoyable. It allows you all to have a voice and have fun laughing or crying together.

It's your journey and your story.

Let's Begin

So, where do ideas for poetry come from? Well, almost anywhere. Some of our best poetry came from quotes we found in places such as news articles, literature, shop names . . . Sometimes this happened by accident in our sessions together when one of us would suddenly say, "Wow, that would make a good poem." That topic or idea would then become the starting point for our writing, which we would share when we connected again. What was interesting was that each of us would take such varied approaches to the topic, so it appeared our poetry came from very different places. There were four voices from four diverse viewpoints, all of equal value. You will see throughout the topics that we have examples of the different approaches.

Here's Your First Activity

- Flip through some magazines, papers, books or any other source that you have available or takes your fancy.
- Make a list of short quotes from these. These can be one or two words or up to a couple of lines.

For example:

    What were the news headlines this morning? Example: "It makes me feel like I do not exist."

    Have you seen some unusual shop names? Example: Shoe shop called "Obsession."

What about famous poems? Example: "Annabelle Lee" by Edgar Allan Poe.

    "For *the moon never* beams without bringing me dreams."

Music lyrics that you can't get out of your mind. Example: "The Dangling Conversation" with lyrics by Paul Simon and Art Garfunkel.

> "Like a poem poorly written
> We are verses out of rhythm
> Couplets out of rhyme
> In syncopated time"

As individuals or as a group, choose one of the quotes and quickly write down anything that comes to mind about the quote you selected.

    This can be:
- Words
- Angles to explore
- Places/ways to research
- Experiences
- What your quote might be referring to

This is just a starting point, so don't get too detailed. Write just enough so you don't lose an idea you might want to use.

This is how we explored possibilities before beginning to write our poems. So put this aside now . . . don't lose it! We are sure you will come to understand why you have done this activity and find it useful later.

Topic 1: Gardens

How did this topic come about?

We have all been in gardens, big and small. Visually, they are full of life and colour and most of us will have pleasant memories of them. Even unpleasant memories, such as ant bites, weeds or prickles can generate stories. The people we have shared gardens with are also important. Helping a grandmother weed or stopping our child from picking grandpa's prize snapdragons will emerge from our memories when we think of gardens.

In times of stress, many of us retreat to our gardens and local parks to help us find peace. Research is now showing what most of us already knew. A walk in the garden, the park, the bush or the forest can have a positive impact on our sense of well-being.

The world of poetry and art is full of gardens and that can be an interesting starting point for this topic. If you have access to the internet, then a search will find you lots of material, or a trip to the local library can help.

Here are a few examples of poems written by the authors.

One Day at Middle Head

Sitting in the open air
Surrounded by native bush
The sun pushed through the misting rain
And I felt the peaceful hush.

Woven through the grey green leaves
Bottlebrush spread their gold
Rainbow parrots fluttered their wings
Ancient stories to be told.

Old rock walls, signs of fortification
Of a much earlier time
And all the while the little green plants
Pushing up through the rime.

Civilisations of another age
Can't help but come to mind
Here in this, the coastal garden
A special one of its kind,

With views to the Pacific Ocean
And of bays and harbour blue,
Grasses and trees, flora and fauna,
Such peace to share with you.

—Jude Comerford

Why did I write this poem?

I wrote this while reminiscing about time spent in this beautiful area during a short getaway with my daughter, enjoying the surroundings of bush and birds and quiet, yet so close to the city and its noisy environment.

A few words about the style and structure of the poem

This lyrical poem is a private expression of emotion by the poet. Lyrical poetry can be highly musical, often featuring rhyme and rhythm. This poem captures the atmosphere of the bush and tells of the timelessness of the land. It has five verses with every second and fourth line rhyming. The choice of words creates a visual scene for the reader.

Antlions

Under our house, the sunlight slants through the slats
reaching long fingers into the cool darkness.
The dirt is cold on my toes, fine like sand.
I sift it through my palms and then move
into the darkest corner I can find.

I search the dirt, for little cones upside down.
They cluster by the wooden posts holding up the house,
Each cone different. Some deep and wide as my little hand,
the dirt finer than under my feet.
Silently I watch, waiting for little claws to push up through the dirt.

I pull the feather of grass from my mouth, softly tickling
the edge of the largest cone. A little slide of dirt
trickles down. I hold my breath.
Too much dirt and I will bury my prey!
Too small an avalanche and my quarry will never feel the vibrations.

Another trickle and I see it now!
From the apex at the bottom of the trap, two tiny jaws
and then, the head comes out and flicks sand where the imaginary ant
slips to its untimely death.

I have watched my brother drop live ants
onto the slippery slide of the ant lion's hole.
I have seen those jaws clamp down upon the ant and
I have quietly slipped away
to cry silently behind the choko vine.

—Sue Elmes

Why did I write this poem?

Growing up in a time when we were often sent outside and told to amuse ourselves, our yard and the dark spaces under our house were our first playgrounds. I don't remember who taught us to tease antlions from their little ant traps, but it was a great way to pass the time.

A few words about the style and structure of the poem

The poem itself is a narrative—it tells a story. It is free verse. It is also a lyrical poem because it captures the emotion, curiosity and sadness of a small child.

Where Roses Grow

Tis hither the scent of roses sweet abounds
Their beauty draws the dames of Brookfield here
With baskets, snips and gloves they may be found
Choosing vibrant blooms from the gardens near

A paradise of perfume and colour bright
A gift of love and generosity
A place of beauty and sensory delight
A haven of joy and reciprocity

Gather what you need and leave a fair due
Tis a give and share all social care space
Wish all the world could glow in similar hue
Of this nurture, love for life and grace

Give beauty to the inward soul, in sum
The outward and the inward self be one [1]

—Dianna Fames

---

[1] Quote from Socrates

Why did I write this poem?

I was inspired to write this poem by a wonderful garden in Brookfield. There is a resident who has turned his property into a rose garden that is open for anyone who wants to sit amongst the roses or pick a bunch to take home. His sole purpose is to make people happy. The beauty of the roses and the owner's spirit enabled me to wrestle with the poetic form of sonnet writing.

A few words about the style and structure of the poem

This poem is an example of a Shakespearean sonnet. It incorporates the theme of nature, a specific rhyme scheme and a specific rhythm, which we will talk about in Topic 5.

Home on the Hill

The old Queensland home sits tall on the hill
Rich with love, memories, and hope.
Rain falls gently as I gaze through the window
A vista slowly revealed.

Trees dotted randomly on thirsty grass plains
Soften the landscape and welcome the rain
Bovine creatures rise slowly from slumber
Energised, by the cooling gift of the rain.

They chew tender grass now covered in raindrops
Throats no longer parched, wide backs refreshed.
Dirt roads previously unnoticed now glisten wet
And wind to places unknown.

All around now peaceful, calm and serene
Glad I stopped for a moment and soaked up the scene.

—Kate Kennedy

Why did I write this poem?

The poem is not about my garden but my friend's property at Helidon. Inspiration came when I was visiting her. I was just sitting there looking out of the window when it started to rain. I picked up a napkin and began to write. As usual, it was only a framework, but as I thought more about it later, it just flowed. She has the poem framed on her wall. I never expected that and am very chuffed. I recently visited the home on the hill after the rains, and it has transformed into a lush green vista. Another opportunity to write. You too can write something special for a friend... the best gift you can give them.

A few words about the style and structure of the poem

This poem is free verse, but you will notice that there are some rhymes that just flowed naturally.

Activities

This is the first topic you will write about. You need to take as much time as needed to complete the activities below. Do it over as many sessions as you like.

This topic has four activities. It is up to you and/or your group to decide how many activities you choose to explore. You may even want to come up with your own ideas.

First Activity

Gardens can be vastly different, impacted by climate, the type of soil and the energy people have to spare for gardening.

- Individually, write down anything that comes to mind about gardens. Think of all the different aspects of gardens, not just the flowers, trees and shrubs. Consider the grass, dirt, insects, compost and tools.
- Share what you have written with the group.
- As people share, capture any ideas or words that inspire you. Shape those words and phrases into a collection of words that roughly resembles a short unstructured poem.
- Share if you wish.

Homework (For your own exploration)

Research some poetry, artwork or articles about gardens.

- What stands out for each of you?
- How can different ideas stimulate inspiration for others as well as ourselves?

Ongoing Activity

Think about a famous garden you have been to or seen. Was it in spring or autumn? Was it covered with snow or an outback desert?
- Think about how they made you feel.
- Immerse your mind in gardens.
- Write a list of all the feelings this has generated for you.

Keep this information as it will be helpful when writing your final poem about gardens.

Ongoing Activity

Using everything you and the group have recorded, including all your earlier work, begin writing your poem.

If you have a strong idea or focus, start with that. It is also natural to have no real idea what to write. When this happens, consider sitting or meeting in a garden with a coffee shop or just have a picnic and let the inspiration come.

If you are still struggling, consider writing a paragraph. Condense it to shape your poem.

For example	This might become
"I walked past the roses and their scent drifted past me. The rotunda rose before me and my mind dragged me back to picnics with the family."	I walked past the roses Scent drifting past Dragging me back. Up rose the rotunda and before me, my family Sitting on a rug. The band played on.

"I was sitting on the lounge watching my dog lying on the floor. His back legs were sticking straight out the back of him and he had a big fat tummy because he had just had his dinner. He keeps me company and as a result I am never lonely. My heart suddenly burst with love for him."

"Every winter we are grateful for the old wood heater that sits in the middle of the lounge room. Although it can be smokey and dusty, the warmth and the glow that it radiates brings such a welcome comfort for weary bodies such as ours."

I watched my dog
Flat out on the floor
Contented round tummy
Back legs poking out.
My old furry friend
Loneliness averted
I love you, my chum.

Old wood heater
Warm and glowing
Take your time to burn.

Old wood heater
Smokey, dusty
It's winter, it's your turn.

Old wood heater
Welcome comfort
Our weary bodies yearn.

Topic 2: Childhood Memories

How did this topic come about?

Memories from childhood can remind us of a time when we didn't have the responsibilities of being an adult. For many, childhood can seem a simpler, happier world.

Of course, not every part of our childhood was happy. Thinking of the simple pleasures we enjoyed can help us feel more alive as we slip back into that world.

A sunny day in the park or the backyard with friends, or a visit to the beach, a river or a creek can remind us of laughter. The feel of melted ice cream on our chins, prickles, splinters, growling dogs and grazed knees were all part of the adventures of a time long gone.

The Bush up the Back

Our street was a cul-de-sac some posh folk might say
A dead end we called it 'cos we weren't that way
This dead end gave way to wild Aussie bush
Our playground where time went by in a whoosh.

Don't go in too far, Mum said . . . finger waving
Who knows what's in there that could be waiting?
And be back before dark, or you'll answer to Dad
He is kind and funny but don't get him mad.

We built cubbies from sticks their roofs made with branches
And a dubious swing where we took our chances
Though a mix of races we played without care
No differences noticed when there in our lair.

As the years went by the cubbies laid bare
And the street became quiet . . . the silence so rare
As it happened our playground was high on a hill
A posh new estate now but memories live still.

—Kate Kennedy

Why did I write this poem?

Someone said to me one day, "Remember the bush up the back when we were growing up?" A flood of memories came back in an instant. I was reminded of the gap between the have and have nots in the neighbourhood as well as the racism that existed not between the children playing together but between some of their parents. I look forward to the day when it is stamped out forever. You can inspire others and make a difference in the world through your poetry.

A few words about the style and structure of the poem

The poem used a set rhyme structure. In each verse the first and the second line rhyme and the third and fourth line rhyme; which is termed AABB.

My Granny's Garden (From the Map of My Childhood Days)

The map of my childhood days
lies dormant beneath my chubby hands.
Paper crisp and new, unblemished
by my moving feet, too young as yet to
move beyond the confines of our yard.
No knowledge yet to trace the contours of the streets,
the gullies or the bush land of our neighbourhood.

My legs slowly lengthen and my balance steadies,
my gaze looks up and the map grows clearer,
the driveway and the squeaky gate, the hedge
that guards my granny's house
and then the corner.

This is the place where dragons lurk
waiting for me to fall off the map.
I look behind. The hill looms over us,
covered in bush.
I feel quite brave to come this far.

To the north, the roller coaster road
rushes up and down into the distance.
Quickly, quietly I slip through the hedge,
walk past the gerberas, the lilies and the staked-up dahlias,
to hide in the old chook pen,
or behind the choko vine to watch the snails and lizards.

The adults, casual in their care,
would watch and question your choice of route
if you stumbled across their path.
"Does your mother know where you are?
"Don't pick the flowers! Go back to your place."

A gentle push and my feet would move
to the soft dry dirt under the house
so I could tease the antlions with a wisp of grass
or flood the sandpit and make rivers, streams and mountain ranges
that even my legs couldn't conquer
or sit on the bottom step and let the sun warm my cold legs.

Dreaming, imagining the day I'd turn the corner
and follow the street until I reached the end.

—S<small>UE</small> E<small>LMES</small>

Why did I write this poem?

This poem began as a series of stories about my childhood. I have always been fascinated by maps, early map-makers and early navigators. I imagined my childhood home and neighbourhood as an ancient map that I gradually explored as I grew, filling in the features on the map. In fact, we lived beside two grannies and once I was able to move further, those were the first gardens I explored. When we formed our little poetry group, I played around with turning the stories into poems, which would all form a work called "The Map of My Childhood Days."

A few words about the style and structure of the poem

This poem, like most of mine, is in free verse, with no rhyming scheme. For me, the most important aspect of a poem is the selection of words and the rhythm they create. What I want to create is an image, both emotional, and hopefully, visual of my childhood. In the first couple of lines, can you imagine the crisp paper of the map being scrunched up by chubby toddler hands? I hope in the fourth verse you can see the hilliness of the road and feel my urgency as I slip through the hedge.

At My Grandmother's House

Tick-tock
Sound of the chiming clock
Awake and asleep
At my grandmother's house

Pink jelly
Made with canned milk
Sweet and wobbly
At my grandmother's house

Pencils, paper
Lots of drawing
Pictures of dreams
At my grandmother's house

Windows rattle
South wind blows
Lace curtains flutter
At my grandmother's house

Warm, cosy
Coal fire sparkles
Safe and tucked in
At my grandmother's house

—Dianna Fames

Why did I write this poem?

I was inspired by Elizabeth Bishop (American poet) to write this poem. She lost her father at a very early age, and her mother spent most of her life in a mental asylum. Her childhood and early life were spent with her grandmother as I did.

A few words about the style and structure of the poem

The simple choice of language creates a wonderful atmosphere. Each verse looks the same, which is a repetitive verse pattern. Each verse is based on a particular sense, i.e., sound, taste, sight and feeling. The repetition of the last line in each verse creates the deep sense of place I found at my grandmother's house.

Christmas Holidays

These are the days that I love
Stretching ahead in my mind
Like one endless daisy chain
Oh, I can't wait to get to the beach.

Mum puts the big round basket
Right in the middle of the table
Soon it fills up with picnic goodies
Bread rolls, garlic sausage and the salad stuff.

Then onto the bus with all our gear
Cries of "I can see the sea" resound
Soon we bag our possie at our favourite spot
On the "Green patch" of grass fronting the sand.

Sharp sting of seawater on skin
Then out onto sand so white,
Sun on our legs as we kneel to build castles,
Decorate with shells from the shoreline.

A grown-up voice calls from the grassy patch
"Lunch." We settle on rugs under trees.
Mothers butter and fill our bread rolls,
Crisp on the outside, so soft to the bite.

No swimming 'til "lunch has gone down" is the rule,
So off we trek around the rocks,
Jump over glassy pools,
To look into sun-filled depths.

Topic 2: Childhood Memories

We seek treasures, crabs and tiny fish,
Return with scratched feet, trailing delicate pink seaweed.
Back into the water for more noisy fun
Before we lie down to dry in the sun.

Time for afternoon tea, scones and jam, cornflake cookies,
Orange cordial and Granny Smith apples.
One little voice says, "Can we have ice creams?"
And older children are sent to buy them.

The day starts to cool, time for showers and change.
To the dressing sheds, swimmers to shorts, skirts, shirts.
Sunburn begins to bite, mothers allot tasks
As they pack up the remains of the day.

"Home now, let's go or we'll miss the bus."
Glad to do so, we are tired and happy.
One daisy gone from the daisy chain,
But still plenty more to come.

Memories of the sight of the sea,
Smell of salt on skin,
The plaintive screech of seagulls,
Sand filtering through fingers.

Our mothers quietly chatting,
Free from family chores
Enjoying the day as we do
The memory will always mean so much.

—Jude Comerford

Why did I write this poem?

One of the topics our group decided to use was "childhood memories." An important memory for me is a day at the local beach at Balmoral on the coast in Sydney. It lies between North Head and Middle Head on the harbourside where Middle Harbour begins its way inland.

Many a day was spent at Balmoral, together with cousins and aunts, mothers and a grandmother or two. These for me are indelible memories and my poem is addressing just one of many special occasions at this harbourside beach.

A few words about the style and structure of the poem

This is unstructured/free verse. It is lyrical in that it expresses the excitement of the childhood ritual of going to the beach with family. I have used keywords to express the feel of the beach.

Activities

Group Discussion

As a group, have a general discussion about the childhood you remember.

Share the ideas and note how similar or different they are.

Activity One

- "Paint" a picture in your mind of your childhood. What did you see, hear, taste, touch and smell?
- Now, write a single line based on one or more of the senses.
- Share the line you have written with the group.
- Was each other's experiences similar or different?
- After the discussion, each person should write five more lines relating to your childhood.

For Example

"I taste the honeysuckle as I pull the flower apart
My feet press firm on the metal pedals
The smell of Mum's cooking drew me home
I hear the steamroller grind over the gravel
I see the silver beet and chokos and I groan"

Activity Two

- Select a partner and share your initial work. Offer some positive feedback.
- Now, go back to your work and rearrange the lines; add or delete words or ideas until there is something more pleasing

to you.
- Polish your work. You now have an example of a free-verse poem to share.

Another fun option

A variation is to write a stanza based on each sense with each group member contributing a line.

We came up with the following verse for taste:

"I taste the honeysuckle as I pull the flower apart,
The juices of the red apple exploded in my mouth,
My granny's cake dripped with lemony butter."

Yes, it needs polishing, but it is fun to play!

Where did you go in your discussion of childhood? Were you drawn back to special places and times where you smell and touch your memories?

Preparation for your next meeting

Pick another place from your childhood. List words and phrases that describe what this place looked like:
- What did you see?
- What did you smell?
- What colours did you see?
- What noises did you hear?
- What temperature did you feel (windy, dusty, etc.)?
- Who else was there?

- Were you allowed to be there or was it a secret place hidden from adults?
- Was there food, lollies, ice cream, etc.?

Using what you have recorded, write a poem to share at your next session.

Topic 3: Obsession

How did this topic come about?

Where does one get inspiration? Some leave it to chance. Sometimes it is a word that stands out on a page you happen to be reading or a picture in a magazine or a book. For us, this topic emerged when we were chatting about someone's favourite shoe shop. Everyone then started to think about their obsession and, hey presto, we were on a roll.

So, where to now? We looked up the meaning of the word.

Obsession is defined as "The state of being obsessed with someone or something."

Can you think of words or phrases that mean the same as obsession? Did you come up with passion, enthusiasm, a "bee in one's bonnet."

Take Covid as an example. The pandemic has become a worldwide obsession and has given us time to reflect as we try to make sense of our global dilemma. It has brought out the best and worst in people. So many bees in so many bonnets, hovering, buzzing . . . obsessing.

You can express or vent your concerns, views and opinions on a controversial topic through poetry. Ask yourself: What am I trying to

express? Is it hope for the future, encouragement for those in need or just plain anger at the situation? How can I get my point across so it makes an impact?

Laughter is such good medicine. A funny poem can lift spirits. Pam Ayres, the English poet, is a great example of this method.

So, what's your obsession or the bee in your bonnet?

The following poems provide examples for you to consider.

Temptress in the Window

She's small and round with a gentle wobble,
A creamy complexion and face dusted brown.
I pass where she sits each day in the window
Alluring, fresh, tempting, and sweet.

She's no good for you, everyone tells me
But temptation wins out, logic now gone.
I creep closer and closer like a naughty child
My desire increasing and taking hold.

The silence is broken by a distant girl's voice.
"What's your guilty pleasure, there's lots of choice?"
Urgently I tell her my heart's desire
And she gives it willingly with a cheeky smile.

I devour it all . . . soothing to my soul,
But it's over too soon and I long for some more.
The voice asks again, "Is there anything else?"
"Yes, another custard tart please, there's one left on your shelf."

—Kate Kennedy

Why did I write this poem?

When someone came up with the topic of obsession, I couldn't think of anything other than my grandchildren. But, driving past our local bakery in Yeronga, I had yet another craving for a custard tart. I realised I actually had a battle within myself every time I drove by not to stop and get one. When, at times, they had sold out, I found myself somewhat disappointed. Maybe I will give them my poem one day. It is a brave thing for anyone to do as you never know whether they will be stoked, as my friend was, or couldn't give a toss and think you are a bit weird.

A few words about the style and structure of the poem

This is an unstructured/free-verse poem. However, did you notice the unintentional rhyme in the third verse? The rhythm is constant, four beats to a line. The poet's yearning for the last tart overcame her desire to be good.

My Reading Obsession

I finish the book. I sigh. Things wait!
Washing, garden, shopping.
Should I tidy the house?
But wait, this author has another book!
I'll just download it
But I'll read it later.
Interesting cover, I like the description!
Oh, it tidied up that character.
Does he/she/they find happiness?
I carry my iPad to the laundry.

I put the sheets in.
Fifty-nine minutes if I use warm water.
That's hygienic.
I can read while I pick up the sh..stuff
the husband/partner/s/kids/grandkids/dog/cat left on the floor.

Exhaustion sets in.
Tea/coffee/organic/probiotic/caffeine-less/beverage!
Sigh! Tastes terrible but feels good.
Dinner? Oh yes, a roast—two hours if I time it right.
Or a slow cooked casserole with couscous?
I read in between peeling/chopping/macerating the onion.
Sheets in the dryer; on low, don't want to kill the elastic.

The unhappiness of the main character is evident.
Open the wine!
Slop some in the pan, pour a glass.
The dog/kids/grandkids/random elderly relative needs a walk!
An hour to go. I grab the kindle, plus pet(s)/person(s) and

off to the park/dog park/playground.
Read and walk, no tripping, bumping into or losing is achieved.
Safely home.

Bone for animal, TV on for child/children/relative/partner.
Prop up iPad as I stir the gravy/pasta/jus/whatever.
More wine, microwave the broccoli/peas/beans/corn.
Fibre is important.

NO READING AT THE TABLE!

What, says child, scrunching her comic/elderly aunt, clutching her paper/partner holding a briefing paper! Dog is happy/cat is hiding.

What the hell do you think I have been doing all day I shout!
Do you think I get to sit and read all day!
What the fu..fennel do you think I do?

Now tell me what you're grateful for,
what you got for your test/spelling/presentation?
Did your boss/teacher/CWA meeting edit that brilliant piece I helped you write?

Oh! I give up. Just eat up and get off to your rooms.
I need some time to read!

—SUE ELMES

Why did I write this poem?

As you can see, this poem is a stream of consciousness based on my obsession with reading. I have always loved reading, and this has become more of an obsession as I age. On a bad day, I can read almost all day, fitting essential tasks in around my reading. It is not unknown for me to have several books going at one time. A romance, a mystery, a non-fiction on an historical topic and something that will put me to sleep!

A few words about the style and structure of the poem

I hope the slightly manic pace of the poem comes across to the reader. Did you notice the inconsistency in the number of lines to a verse? This is an example of totally free verse. Despite attempts to polish the poem, I found it hard to make the poem more literary, and in the end, I just gave in to the frenetic nature of the topic. It has always been a rule in our house not to read at the table as that was for conversation, both serious and absurd. But this is my imagination having fun with taking my obsession to its limits.

Purchasing Blues

Deliah's gone shopping
She needs a new top
An obsession she hopes
One day will stop.

Much effort entailed
In avoiding assistants
She darts between racks
As a way of resistance.

Arms full of garments
She never will wear
Holed up in the change room
Helps ease purchase despair.

Nothing quite fits
And the pressure is mounting
She's been there for hours
On a purchase she's counting.

Then just as she's leaving
Spots a rack over there
Stretchy, large, black tops
Buys two, leaves, minus despair.

Episode over
Disaster allayed
She admires her purchases
And notes that she's overpaid!

—Dianna Fames

Why did I write this poem?
I had to think about why I wrote "Purchasing Blues." Then, I remembered it started as a humorous short story set in Covid times when frequenting shopping centres required the wearing of masks and was a risky undertaking, made even worse if shopping was a compulsive obsession. The story version lay around for some time until I revamped it into a poem.

A bit about the style and structure of the poem
It is written in verse using rhyming with a set number of lines per verse.

Birthright

Maybe, if you wanted to,
you could call me "quaint."
That's what a girl at school had said,
When at thirteen I had bought a little pair of blue booties
for my newborn baby cousin.

First, I had bristled
But soon rose above it, that particular word.
Thinking on it now, perhaps that could explain
why I had always liked collecting things.

But no, that was stretching the word "quaint" too far.
Why should I explain? From an early age
I liked to gather my mother's old magazines,
stack them neatly beside my big old wardrobe.
I ask that of myself now.

Did it throw light on the fact
that I would never think of disposing of anything given to me as a gift,
or something that held a memory of a holiday at the beach, for instance,
jars of shells as evidence of happy times?

The stones and rocks I loved to pick up
And place on my window sill.
No, this was not "quaint," this was "obsessive."
I had never before given it a name. I had an obsession.

That's probably why I couldn't hang back
when near an antique shop or op shop of any description,
buying a pair of old candlesticks, an old vase.
These made me wonder. Who had owned them?
Who had fashioned them in the first place?

This obsession of mine stretched to clothes,
I realised with some shame. I promised myself then,
I must offer to others what no longer fitted.
Nothing new, not ever. A New Year resolution!
With every fresh thought now, I felt invigorated, quite "normal."

But in the next thirty seconds I reminded myself—
Still, my birthday flowers, bunches of them, drying on the balcony!
Did I need these reminders of a joyful day?

Perhaps not, but the natural burnished colours of them I loved.
Maybe they would fit in somewhere inside, if I just moved a few
things around.
Then I faced the inevitable. Call it what I or you or anyone else
might.
Quaint one, clutterer, hoarder, obsessive.
I couldn't remember ever being any other way.
But at a late age now, I have come to terms with myself.
That other girl at school was a clever one to put a name to it, I think.
That's what she had said, "quaint."

I like "obsessive" better.
Yes, quite right, I always was, and still happy to be so.
It's who I am.

You'll wonder now what on earth
all this has to do with a pair of blue bootees
which started me off.
I wonder and shrug.

—Jude Comerford

Why did I write this poem?

Funny how tiny things said to us or similar remarks made to others often stay somewhere in the mind and reassert themselves at strange times throughout people's lives. This is about one of those times.

A few words about the style and structure of the poem

This verse is completely unstructured/free verse. The length of the lines varies according to the feeling or situation as experienced by me at the time.

Activities

Definitions of Obsession:

"The state of being obsessed with someone or something."

"An idea that continually preoccupies or intrudes on a person's mind."

Now, use the following questions to explore some thoughts and ideas about "obsession."

- What is your obsession? (Name it)
- Describe how it makes you feel.
- How does it make you act?

What words would you use to describe the obsession? Examples: all-consuming, guilty pleasure/secret, enthusiasm, fascination, preoccupation.

What would you say to someone else about the obsession? Examples: I can't help myself, I am a slave to my obsession, I am drawn inexplicably.

Write a short story about it. Use some of your responses to the questions above if you like or just write freely.

Now, put that story into a poem using any of the techniques you have learnt so far.

Don't forget to give yourself a pat on the back. You have come a long way.

Topic 4: Illnesses and Personal Crisis

How did this topic come about?

Everyone experiences times in their lives that are difficult and challenging. It can be hard to make sense of the world at these moments and often for a long time afterwards. It can seem as though our thoughts circle endlessly around in our minds.

Writing about these moments can help us to slow down enough to begin the process of healing or moving forward.

Poetry is perfect for doing this as it can quickly capture the thoughts that are associated with your distress: things such as panic, anxiety, catastrophising and the what ifs.

Writing about personal issues, a family crisis, illness, anxiety and emotions can be a very private experience and is not always something that a writer wants to share. However, working with a group of trusted friends can be part of the healing process.

You can meet with your group over coffee or wine to generate ideas, play with words or explore potential themes. However, writing your poem may best be done in private and only shared if you feel comfortable.

The Scar

The scar runs deep
No one can see it;
It dwells in a dark place
Dormant . . . waiting.

Without warning it rises
Gate crashing happy times;
She relives it in silence
The torment still strong.

She's beautiful and poised
Everyone says;
Nothing fazes that girl
Wish I was like her.

The invisible scar
Returns to its den;
The ruse continues
Till it's triggered again.

—Kate Kennedy

Why did I write this poem?

Have you had painful memories flood back into your mind? It could be something you see others doing or sometimes, out of the blue, it just "gets you." For me, it was a crisis that happened forty years ago, yet it still comes up to "bite me" from time to time. It is lurking as the poem suggests. Others don't see it from the outside; they just see what I let them see. Nonetheless, the scar remains. It is a reminder that most people don't get off scot-free from life's blows, and though they appear confident from the outside, they battle their demons within.

A few words about the style and structure of the poem

This is unstructured, free flowing as the trigger itself. The short verses underpin the pain the girl experiences from time to time.

Lost World Dreaming

Quietly on the chair she sits wrapped in a blanket barely wakeful
Hearing water swiftly bubbling,
Around her feet the quail slip quietly unaware
She sees them moving from the grass to reach the water.

Above her head the trees are moving in the wind off mountains coming
In the sky the clouds are rushing
In the branches over water the crested hawks are mating loudly
Building nest with noisy screeches
Unaware she lies beneath them
Willing every cell to listen to her demand for action.

She sits;
Wrapped warm in meditation while he chops the wood
and heats the water
Life made simple in a mountain cabin.

Possum sleeping in the rafters
Air freely moving through cabin walls
Fire burning at one end
A bed two chairs and one small lantern.

They talk of fears and possibilities
A future that may not be granted
Of wasted chances and the complications of living in a zone of fear
Of trepidation and new ways of seeing.

The meaning of life in a drop of water previously
eluded understanding.
Now she knew what he was saying
Now she knew the glint of sun on needle leaves
Or water dripping off the branches
A blade of grass with cobwebs glistening in the early morning rain.
All could reveal the complex web of life and grieving.

Ten years on she still remembers the quiet of the mountain hut
Isolation and introspection
The loneliness of such an illness
Shutting others out for now
Strength conserved to go on living fighting breathing eating
No energy to spare for others.

—Sue Elmes

Why did I write this poem?

This poem was written at a time when I was reflecting on my experience of having chemotherapy for Non-Hodgkin's lymphoma in my early forties. At the time, I learnt how to meditate and used it as a way to escape the pain and isolation of the treatment and the constant worry. Since then, I have meditated on and off whenever I need it to find calm and reduce stress and anxiety. It is a wonderful tool in this crazy world!

The reference to the meaning of life in a drop of water comes from Patrick White's novel, *The Tree of Man*. When I first read this book in my late teens, I didn't understand the author's point. But, I came to see that light shining through a glob of spit could beautify and encapsulate the meaning of life: the small and often beautiful experiences of daily life, a raindrop on a Nasturtium leaf, a smile, a ray of sunlight, a bubble floating above the sink of dishes.

A few words about the style and structure of the poem

The poem is in unstructured/free verse. I rarely use rhymes, but I always look for the rhythm of the words and if they will sound pleasing to the reader. I believe poems should be read out loud. This allows you to hear the rhythm that is vital in creating atmosphere. In this poem, a mood of lingering sadness is juxtaposed next to the beauty of the natural world.

As the writer of this poem, I believe you will find there is no set rhythm. It changes to reflect the mood and imagery. There are times when a line moves quickly and others where the rhythm slows right down. Consider the first two lines of the poem. The first moves slowly and is long, while the second is short and moves swiftly.

The imagery in the poem revolves around the hut, the birds and the drop of water.

I have tried to include words where the sound echoes the sense. Examples: "swiftly bubbling" and "noisy screeches." This is known as onomatopoeia.

Eleventh Night Hour

How deafeningly silent you are
So still
All action suspended
Deep sleep has descended for many, but not all
A small black dog quivers with dream trembles beside me
I comfort him and pat him gently
I am awake in a still life photograph, a scene of my life surrounds me
Boxes, bags, books, mess everywhere
Not bothered to tidy, I sit and stare into the eleventh night hour.

The night is my sunrise,
My dawn of imagination
Mind floating in and out of time
Can a fragile self collapse and fall,
Then get back up again?
It happens in the eleventh night hour
With Venus in her orbit,
Owls calling from their tree.
It is only in this hour
That the moon glows back at me.

—Dianna Fames

Why did I write this poem?

The poem was written in two parts. The first verse was written eight months ago and is based on my actual experience sitting on the couch late at night with my dog. I was acutely aware of the deafening silence. The second verse was written more recently, and the shortness of the lines takes the reader one image at a time reflecting on the beauty of the night. Each line is important as together they build the atmosphere.

A few words about the style and structure of the poem

This poem is an example of free, unstructured verse. The long lines slow the reader down and create a dream-like pace. The shorter lines build momentum. The imagery creates a strong visual that you can see and feel. It draws the reader into the poet's experience. Example: "The night is my sunrise, my dawn of imagination."

Topic 4: Illnesses and Personal Crisis

The Countdown

Radiotherapy number fifteen of thirty.
Halfway through, second half starts Monday.
Follow Routine. Shoes off, shirt off,
Lie on table.

Restraint on, then clipped to the table
Head held in place. He hates it.
Can't move, pinned down, nose sticks out,
Protective mask on.
His eyes glare through the cut-outs.

Deep breath now, thick saliva
At the back of his throat,
Needs to swallow. Can't move.
Can't manage it.

A drowning sensation, wants to aspirate.
Just manages to swallow.
Breathe, just breathe, just breathe.
Should have taken that Valium.

Nurse Donna knows how he feels,
She's so good, they all are.
He has a feeling
There is worse to come.

This whole treatment is to kill
Microscopic cancer cells,
Worthwhile! He keeps telling himself.
Table slides under the machine.
Scans today. It will be longer.

They leave the room. Alarm goes off.
The "zap" is about to happen.
Minutes pass. What are they doing?
Massive machine moves. Scans performed.

Zapping lasts fifteen minutes.
He sees himself reflected,
Distorted in the glass of the machine
As it circles around his neck.
Is that really him? He closes his eyes as though
Scared by the sight of himself—his own face.

Dozing now.
The machine makes its second, then third pass.
He dreams of his new lady. How lucky he is.
He is a cancer patient. There are no pretensions.
No explanations necessary
Two down to earth people in love.

He appears calm waking from his daze.
Completes his routine. Shoes on, shirt on, tuck in.
Thank you to the nurses, "See you Monday."
Makes haste to The Pineapple
For a beer on the way home.

Past the halfway mark, fifteen treatments to go.
Feeling blessed for many, many reasons.

—Jude Comerford

Why did I write this poem?

These are the verses that evolved from my son's story of one of his cancer treatments. It helps me to understand just a little of what he experienced. It may help others who are going through their own health challenges and/or providing support for family and friends in the same situation.

A little bit about the style and structure of the poem.

The poem is written in free verse. The short lines and phrases emphasise the urgency of the situation and the strict routine of the medical procedures. This highlights the clinical nature of the entire experience. This is contrasted with the emotional content of the poem as expressed by the dreams of his new lady and how fortunate he feels.

Activities

With sensitive topics, it is important to think about how to structure the activities so they suit your group. If you know each other really well, you may be happy to share most things, but there should always be the option to write but not share.

Set any boundaries that seem important in your group. For example, you might agree that some topics are too sensitive at the time. For example, "Death" might not be a suitable topic if someone has recently experienced the death of a loved one. "War" might not be suitable if a group member has someone serving in the armed forces.

Activity

Individually write down events, moments, issues that have impacted on you.

Examples: Illness, depression, broken relationship, family member with dementia...

Choose one or two topics from your list and write them on separate pieces of paper. Place them in a container.

Everyone has a turn pulling out a topic. They can put the topic back if they want and select another.

As a group, discuss the topic ensuring all members take a turn if they wish. It doesn't matter if a person has no personal experience of a topic. The idea is to generate information that can be built into a poem later on.

During the discussion, ask each person to write down words, phrases or images that resonate. There is no right or wrong here, so anything that stands out to you is worth putting down.

Alternatively, on a large piece of paper, have one person write up all the words and phrases each person has written down. Individuals then choose the words that are meaningful to them.

Individually arrange the words in your list to form the basic outline of a poem. Feel free to add extra words if it helps, but keep it to a minimum.

For example, if the words included:
- What if
- Fear
- Loneliness
- Paranoia
- Pain
- Hiding away

Rearranging the words might come up with:
What if it's true?
I hide away
In shock and fear.

Loneliness and pain.
Paranoia
What if it's true?

Share the outcome. It is helpful if everyone reads their own as they will bring their emphasis, intonation and emotion to the reading. The group will hear their voice.

Alternative Activity

Prior to the next meeting, research the internet or other resources such as books and magazines. Look for words and phrases on your chosen

topic and bring them along. These can be extracts, poems, short stories, photos, definitions or anything that relates to your chosen topic.

If possible, make copies for each member. Alternatively, email them in advance.

Discuss what you found, i.e.,
- the facts,
- the emotion surrounding the issue.

Each person should underline the phrases, words and ideas that jump out. They might be useful when writing your poem.

Start writing. Remember, we are not aiming at perfection! We are aiming at a grouping of words, phrases and sentences that express what you, as an individual, feel and think about your topic.

After the first attempt, sit back, think and read it out loud to yourself. Over time, rearrange and edit it.

Share your poem at the next gathering.

Topic 5: Shakespeare

How did this topic come about?

Who would have thought that a casual suggestion to try our hands at writing poetry by one of our Poetry Pals would lead into the heady world of Shakespeare and sonnet creation?

Well, it did, and it was so much fun. It came about simply by a random mention of the Western world's most famous poet. We noted that his talent was not only for great play writing but also that of poetry writing, and in particular, sonnets . . . all 154 of them.

A book of Shakespeare's sonnets was dutifully uncovered from a Poetry Pals literary stash entitled "Shakespeare's Sonnets." We were on our way, selecting readings at random, caught up in the rhythmic beat of the sonnet's pulse and immersed in the beauty of its potent, descriptive essence.

Here's a fun fact about Shakespeare. Did you know that Shakespeare added several thousand unique words to the English language and invented the word prefix "un"? Examples: unhappy, undetected, uncoordinated. A quick search on the internet will come up with more fun facts about Shakespeare. It is interesting that we use Shakespeare's words and phrases today. Examples: *puking, vanish* into thin air, there's a method to my madness, wild goose chase, the green eyed-monster, break the ice, wear my heart upon my sleeve. All this when modern English language was only a hundred years old.

Shakespeare in his sonnets chooses to write about the big-ticket themes, the things that impact on all of us. Examples: love, war, mortality, change, aging. Once the topic is identified, he explores the problem and then finds a solution of sorts in the couplet.

We decided to have a go at writing a sonnet, but before we could do so, we had to explore how the poet constructed them. This is a very simplified, introductory immersion into sonnet writing but a great starting point.

- A Shakespearean sonnet always has fourteen lines.
- These fourteen lines are made up of three verses and a couplet (two lines that rhyme with each other).
- Each verse has four lines.
- The sonnet is finished by adding a couplet.

About the Rhythm

The rhythm Shakespeare uses is called Iambic Pentameter. The following example is the first line from Sonnet 73.

That *time*/of *year*/thou *may'st*/in *me*/behold

You will find the emphasis naturally falls on the words in italics. Go ahead and read it out loud. The word Iambic, mentioned earlier, is an unstressed followed by a stressed syllable.

Every line should have five feet in it. In our example, there are five feet.

Examples:
- That *time*—is the first foot
- of *year*—is the second foot and so on

This is what is meant by Pentameter, which comes from the Greek meaning "five."

Note: While this is Shakespeare's rhythm, in his sonnets and his plays, he regularly uses variations on this pattern.

About the rhyme

Shakespeare has a set rhyming pattern in all his sonnets. We will now use Sonnet 73 to explain this to you.

"That time of year thou may'st in me be**hold**
When yellow leaves, or none, or few, do *hang*
Upon those boughs which shake against the **cold**,
Bear ruin'd choirs, where late the sweet birds *sang*."

You can see from the words in bold and italics that **hold** and **cold** rhyme and *hang* and *sang* rhyme. This is referred to as the rhyming pattern "ABAB." If you look at any Shakespearean sonnet, this pattern will be continued as "CDCD" in the second verse, "EFEF" in the third verse and "GG" in the final couplet.

Examples:
CDCD
In me thou see'st the twilight of such **day**,
As after sun set fadeth in the *west*,
Which by-and-by black night doth take **away**,
Death's second self, that seals up all in *rest*.

EFEF
In me thou see'st the glowing of such **fire**

That on the ashes of his youth doth *lie*,
As the death bed whereon it must **expire**
Consum'd with that which was nourish'd *by*.

GG
This thou perceives, which makes thy love more **strong**,
To love that well which thou must leave ere **long**.

After the Pals deconstructed how Shakespeare created his sonnets, we gave it a go. We found it extremely difficult to faithfully follow his sonnet format. When you read our poems you will notice that not every line is Iambic Pentameter and not every rhyme is perfect. You also need to be aware that Shakespeare did not always follow his own rules. So, feel free to break some too!

Hope you enjoy examples of our sonnets.

The Caterpillar

Along the stalk the caterpillar creeps
Armed with false eyes, mimics leaf and vine
Consuming the leaves, its faeces drop in heaps
Upon the path, awaiting eyes like mine.

Under the soil the earthworm digs in its tunnels
Consuming the microbes and breaking up the dirt
Air and water seep into the runnels
Avoiding beetles, birds, they stay alert.

Noisy Miners fighting, squawk for food
Checking the garden for flowers and nectar, chasing
moths in the grass, feathers fly as they feud
With Magpies, Butcherbirds about facing.

Suddenly! the caterpillar dead
The silent worm slips to its earthy bed!

—Sue Elmes

Why did I write this poem?

This poem was written as an exercise in writing a sonnet. The topic for our writing was anything associated with a garden. I saw some caterpillar droppings under a pot and then found the caterpillars. The poem developed from that starting point.

A few words about the style and structure of the poem

The poem is written in a sonnet form of fourteen lines; in this case, made up of three verses (quatrains) and a final two lines (a couplet). The rhythm is Iambic Pentameter. This means I have attempted to have five feet in each line, made up of an unstressed syllable followed by a stressed syllable. If you look at the poem carefully, you will see that like Shakespeare and many other poets, I have quite a few variations in the rhythm.

Shakespeare and other poets also use a set rhyming scheme and I have been more successful with this, but I never find it easy. Sonnets are not something I would usually write. It is more of an intellectual exercise for me. Can you see the places in the poem where the use of rhyme, together with the five feet of Iambic Pentameter, makes the line clumsy when read?

The Time Has Come

The time has come for me to take the plunge.
No more can I be making lame excuses.
My brain filled up—a sodden, sagging, sponge.
The time has come to put an end to ruses.

The time has come to be good and serious
And not behave as if I am a fool.
I do admit I seem somewhat delirious.
The time has come to start to follow the rule.

The time has come to properly follow the law,
To do what I'm told could be the key to all.
From this day forward I will do even more.
The time has come and I shall follow the call

To be a model citizen I will try
So, I'll wear my mask until the day I die.

—Jude Comerford

Why did I write this poem?

The poem signifies the need to obey the rules as set by government health officials during the 2020–2021 pandemic of Covid infection. Did you notice that the reader was only made aware of this in the last two lines? The repeated use of "the time has come" at the beginning and end of each verse indicates my final submission to wearing a mask at all times.

A few words about the style and structure of the poem

This is an attempt at a sonnet in the Shakespearean style. I was able to follow the rhyming pattern of ABAB, CDCD, EFEF and GG, which makes fourteen lines. However, I found the rhythm/beat of Iambic Pentameter restrictive and hard to achieve.

An Invitation to Tea

Come sit with us, William, lend us your ear
Inspire us with your literary brilliance
Our writing for our sake is so very dear
It charges our hearts with love, joy and resilience.

Our fine group is Sue, Jude, Kate K and me
Delving into your sonnets to enhance
Our journey through a Shakespearean spree.
And now to ponder "What is your substance?"

Where of are you made? Say, what is your matter?
Appraise all what's done or said. For my worth, seize
Rather upon great wisdoms to let scatter,
And end with wise words written by Socrates.

Remember what is unbecoming to do
Is also unbecoming to speak of too.[2]

—Dianna Fames

---

[2] Quote by Socrates

Why did I write this poem?

It was purely an exercise attempting to write a sonnet. I may not have succeeded in all instances, but I had a go.

A few words about the style and structure of the poem

The poem is an example of Shakespeare's sonnet style. It is broadly based around our writing group and the shared experience of attempting to write in a variety of poetry forms. By including the quote by Socrates, I have provided a didactic instruction about one of his philosophies. It was common for writers like Shakespeare to use their poems to raise awareness about morals and philosophy.

The Ring

The stones have no value the jeweller blithely said
It's wartime gold... no value there.
Stones just made of glass, why not diamonds instead?
Lots of sparkle and glitter, a great joy to wear.

I held it imagining all that it meant
How it slipped on her finger having waited so long.
Happiness borne of sadness and lament
Dreams of love now rewarded, anguish all gone.

Her Holy Grail, its value immense
The ring symbolising his life had been spared.
Of new beginnings, a world now making sense
They were young and free, their lives now repaired.

I will wear it with pride, something to be treasured
And if anyone asks, reply, "Its value can't be measured."

—KATE KENNEDY

Why did I write this poem?

I was talking to my son about letting go of things that belonged to our loved ones who have passed away. I said that the only thing I had of my mother's were her engagement and wedding rings, which are of no monetary value. He said it was like her Holy Grail as my father had survived the fighting in Europe during World War II and came back to marry her. I was immediately inspired to write a poem that would reflect the true meaning of her engagement ring.

A few words about the style and structure of the poem

As mentioned in the previous poems, this is a sonnet. The rhythm is not perfect, but the rhyme follows the process.

Activity 1

As a group, choose one of the poems from the previous pages. Alternatively, you may wish to select one of Shakespeare's sonnets. You might like to do this activity into two groups with each group taking a different poem.

Deconstruct the poem as follows:
- Count the number of lines. (Did you come up with fourteen?)
- Identify the three verses. (Did you notice each had four lines?)
- Identify the couplet.
- Did the poem identify the issue? Explore the problem and offer a solution.

About the rhythm
- Read the verses out loud emphasising the stressed syllable. This will usually be the second word in each foot.
- Remembering there are five feet to a line, identify each foot. Don't worry if it is not the second word that is emphasised. It could be the first word or the third word.

About the rhyme
- Remember the ABAB concept. In the first verse, identify the rhyming words that are A or B.
- Remember the CDCD concept. In the second verse, identify the rhyming words that are C or D.
- Remember the EFEF concept. In the third verse, identify the rhyming words that are E or F.
- What is the final verse called?

- The couplet has two lines. Identify the rhyming words that are GG.

Activity 2

Choose a topic.

Example: A family gathering.

Brainstorm words that fit the topic. Examples: hot, humid, flies, mosquitoes, chair, beer, wine, whinging, onions.

Go to the internet and find rhyming words for the words you have chosen above. Examples: hot, pot, lot, dot . . .

Write four lines. The first line and the third line will have a rhyming word at the end and the second and the fourth line will also rhyme.

Ensure you have five beats (feet) to the line.

For example:

I sat/on the step/with a beer/in my/**hand**

Sweat/dripped/from my brow/as I/swatted the *fly*

How/could/my friend/even like/this weird **band**

I flung/down my/straw hat/ and / asked/myself *why*?

Homework

You are being asked to write a sonnet on any topic of your choice for presentation at your next meeting. You may wish to work in pairs to complete the task if you find the concept daunting.

Ensure the sonnet comprises:
- Fourteen lines
- Three verses, each with four lines
- A final verse has two lines, that is, the couplet
- The rhythm should have five feet to a line

- Each foot should finish with a stressed syllable
- Rhyme the sonnet as follows:
    a. ABAB in the first verse
    b. CDCD in the second verse
    c. EFEF in the third verse
    d. GG in the final verse (the couplet)

Topic 6: Meditation for Creativity

How did this topic come about?

Writing is a form of meditation. Putting words to paper is a way of making our thoughts, feelings, ideas and concerns more discernible, coherent and manageable.

A social upheaval such as Covid has been a major influencing force in everyone's life. Some of the ways of managing the impact of this ongoing issue have been the writing of personal stories and the sharing of coping strategies. By delving into historic writings on the subject or futuristic predictions of how modern interventions might resolve this dilemma, we gain hope.

Other people's thoughts, feelings, ideas and concerns provide explanations, insights, solace and hope to keep us from going adrift, unsteady and lost.

The Poetry Pals can attest to the fact that any expression of human experience is somehow made very significant when it is wrapped in the eloquence of verse or prose and gifted to the group as a precious insight into the writer's soul.

"Reading poems is a very special kind of mindfulness," says author and anthologist Allie Esiri, author of the book *A Poet for Every Day of the Year*.

The Bali Tree

The Bauhinia tree stood tall
Open branches dangled hither and thither
Precious pink flowers nestled safely
Green leaves framed their glory for all

Branches swayed hypnotically
In the warmth of the gentle Bali breeze
Each delicate flower caressed by the sun
Gave joy to those who admired

It gave shade to all who swim
In the crystal-clear pool below
Without judgement, discrimination or ego
A gift, no payment required

Let's pray for a world such as this
Offering nurture and safety and strength
The lesson is offered by this humble Bali tree
Beginning simply with you and with me

—Kate Kennedy

Why did I write this poem?

I was in Bali a couple of years ago sitting on my hotel balcony overlooking the pool. I was just taking in the scene when the breeze stirred the branches of the tree. It was like the blossoms were waving to everyone who took time to notice or care. Bali welcomes tourists from many countries and the people greet you with broad smiles and a nothing-is-too-much-trouble attitude. How much more inspiration do you need than that? Just look around and you will find it.

A few words about the style and structure of the poem

The style is unstructured with my usual two lines rhyming.

Topic 6: Meditation for Creativity

Staying Afloat with Life-Saving Lines

I cannot cope with Covid
It's driving me insane
Every day the numbers
Every day the blame

Now is not the time to waver
Focus on the strengths and talents that you have
Every person has their struggles in life
Your life has its own agenda to write

If only life was normal
The way it used to be
Our greed has bought us here
To face our destiny

Be sure to tell yourself your kinder truths
Commit to now the past is over
Take stock of the treasures in your life
You are needed to be just as you are

I found it helped to write
Weave anger into hope
Turn the rage to verse, with
My Poetry Pals and cope

See the purpose in every single thing
Choose to seek out joyfulness and kindness
Just take one step at a time through each day
Honour your efforts, all you do and speak

These are my lifelines to keep me afloat
These are the strength words that build my lifeboat

—Dianna Fames

Why did I write this poem?

I merged two poems to strengthen both pieces, as I didn't feel they had enough oomph. I was surprised to see how well they sat together. Like cutting two garments and joining them as one. This began by creating a list of all the wise sayings that would help me stay strong at a time when I feel I'm falling apart and scattered. I prioritised them in order to construct a flow of meaning. Somehow, it just flowed, and from that emerged the final poem.

A few words about the style and structure of the poem

This is an example of an interweaving of rhyming, structured verse and didactic wise sayings as unstructured prose just for fun.

Out the Window

"Steady girl," the woman chided herself,
Wanting to slam the kitchen door,
Electric jug under the tap
She stood there. The water
Flowed into the sink, crammed with dirty dishes.

Some days the kids packed the dishwasher
But not today.
Too chaotic—their dad shouting first thing,
"Come on kids, rise and shine, it's late."
One complaining, "Where are my sports clothes?"

One with an assignment due! In a state about that!
No, today was not a good one, full stop.
Life, it seemed had slipped from her grasp.

Was she happy? Basically.
But darned if she'd clean up the kitchen, again.

Benji the dog sat at her feet, a pivotal presence. She gave him a pat,
Sipped her tea, closed her eyes, took some deep breaths,
Eyes open, she saw the backyard
Through new eyes.
The trampoline in one corner,
The torn mat hanging oddly, but . . .

In the other corner, a different picture,
A tableau of plants, a delightful scene.
Funny, she had never noticed it before.
Pink bougainvillea flowing, star jasmine competing for room,
White azaleas flowering at head height.

The multicoloured petunias
Her mother had planted on her last visit. They were glorious.
There on the other side of the window.
She looked away then around the messy kitchen, sighed
Rushed to the hallway.

Rummaging deeply she found her old watercolour paints and sketchpad,
She picked up a kitchen chair, took it outside.
"Come on, old fella; we're having a day off."
She filled an old jam jar, jammed a hat on head
All set for the morning.

Paint until midday she thought.
Time went quickly.
She put it all aside and
Saw how the weeds had taken over.
She worked in the garden.

Soon too hot for comfort, she filled Benji's water bowl.
Went inside to wash, to tackle the kitchen at last.
Why was it so hard before?
Now done in minutes.
Time then to look out the window, admire her garden work.

It made her smile to see a space. For lavender, she considered.
"Yes," she murmured, excited. "My exclusive view of my very own garden."
She patted Benji, propped her finished painting on the kitchen table
A good day after all, as simple as that.
A good day—she could write a poem about it.

And she did.

—JUDE COMERFORD

Why did I write this poem?

Everyday life with all its chores and challenges can be difficult and depressing. This poem reflects on how painting, working in the garden and growing things can be uplifting. Like meditation, the distraction of natural beauty in a garden can be satisfying to the soul. Attempting to write poetry can do the same no matter the outcome.

A few words about the style and structure of the poem

This poem is unstructured free verse, with each stanza having five lines. The length of the lines and the language reflect the changing mood of the poem. As it moves from annoyance and depression at the beginning of the poem to a much more relaxed and uplifted feeling at the end, the length of lines changes and you can sense the poet's satisfaction with her day.

K'Gari Meditation

I focus on the breath and my mind slips down
Quietly into the rhythm of the world beneath me.
In my mind I see the waves move in and out
Endlessly responding to the tug of the moon's desire.

My mind slips into the cool clear water of the creek
Soft sand beneath, palms above and in the trees nearby
The white cockatoos screech their joy at finding food.
I pause, bringing my mind back to the breath.

And as I slip down into the peace my mind has found,
I smile. Those small glimpses: a bird, a butterfly, a berry;
On a new leaf drops of rain gleam red in the sun,
The flow of water as I lie,
The satinay tree so tall I cannot see the top,
These images float softly to the surface.

And as I meditate, there in the heart of K'Gari,
The red berry hits my head.
I jump and the Narrabeen berries rain down upon me in the creek.
Enough! The cockatoos call loudly.
Look up here and watch us!

—Sue Elmes

Why did I write this poem?

I have practiced meditation for many years. As part of that practice, I often see a peaceful but imaginary place beside the ocean. For many years, I imagined lying in a creek, feeling the soft breeze and hearing the sounds of the coastal trees around me. This is a place of refuge where I can shut out my fears and anxieties while I meditate.

On a recent trip to K'Gari, or Fraser Island, we watched the sulphur-crested cockatoos feeding on red Narrabeen palm berries, dropping as many into Wanggoolba Creek at Central Station as they ate. Cockatoos always appear to enjoy life, playing and fooling around and reminding us that there is joy to be found around us even when times are difficult. My imaginary creek has lately taken on many of the characteristics of Wanggoolba Creek, but the water is warmer!

A few words about the style and structure of the poem

I have used free verse in this poem and was looking for a peaceful meditative mood. Did you notice that all the verses vary in length expressing different images? I love that meditation and nature work together to remind me of the little things that bring peace. The voices of the cockatoos change the energy of the poem and lift me from my meditation into the real world with renewed energy.

Activity 1

Actors, public speakers, singers, balancing acts and anyone who performs on stage uses a method of breathing that in yoga and other physical disciplines is called diaphragmatic breathing or "belly breath." Essentially it means a deep breath into your belly. This serves to calm the body and the mind. Who doesn't want that?

This activity starts with becoming more aware of how important your breathing is to your creative functioning and well-being. The practice of breathing deeply is a simple way to reduce stress and puts you in the frame of mind to be creative.

Now let's use this method to write some poetry.

The Set-Up

Have a pen and paper (or your computer) at the ready.

Elect an individual to lead the short breathing exercise using the following instructions.

Meditation Activity—Belly Breathing

- Settle into sitting comfortably in a chair
- Feet on the floor
- Hands resting gently on the belly above the navel
- Close your eyes
- Begin to breathe in slowly and deeply through your nose
- Feel your in-breath fill and expand your belly
- Breathe out slowly and deeply through your nose
- Feel your belly soften down as you breathe out
- Continue to breathe in this way
- Breathe in and your belly rises

- Breathe out and your belly softens down
- Breathe in/breathe out
- Let all of your attention slip away from the rest of your body and come to rest in the belly space
- Focus on how your warm breath gently soothes your belly space
- Continue to breathe for another five deep, slow breaths
- One breath, two breaths, three breaths, four breaths, five breaths
- Now slowly return to your usual breathing pattern
- Open your eyes
- Move your body a little in the chair
- You are calm and rested

Individual Activity

This activity has hopefully enabled you to be more physically relaxed and ignited your imagination.

Now that you have energised your creativity, draw on any of the techniques in this book and begin to write a poem.

Activity 2 (Individual or group activity)

Choose an image that appeals to you. It may be something in the room or a picture from a magazine.

Place this image where it can be seen.

Spend a minute or two reflecting on this image and jot down some thoughts that come to mind such as:

- What do you see?
- What do you hear?
- What do you feel?

- Did you notice anything in the image that you have never noticed before?
- Did it bring up memories?
- Did it remind you of anything?
- You now have material to begin a poem using any format of your choice.

Author's Concluding Chats

From Kate

Poetry can make me laugh out loud or reach for a tissue to sob into. This has been my journey with the Pals. The elegance and quality of their poetry has been inspiring in several ways. One being the new skills they have taught me but the other, and more importantly, realising how poetry can provide an intimate insight into the rich tapestry of people's lives. I didn't expect to be an integral part of the journey called Playing with Poetry, but I discovered that I had the ability within me to write and even enjoy writing poetry. This has been an extremely uplifting experience and I hope that you, just like me, enjoy your journey as you work through this handbook.

From Jude

When a small group of women decided to start a poetry group, I thought this might be for me and was delighted to be included. Never having written poetry, I am finding there is a lot to learn and is something I have not thought about since school days.

It is fun to be part of the group. My fellow members have become true friends. We were strangers to start with, but through poetry and sharing and learning about it and the writing of it, we have fused a strong bond. The preparation of this handbook, for the purpose of encouraging others to try their hand at writing poetry, has been a journey that has kept me interested and enthusiastic to the very end.

I hope you will find pleasure in reading our poems and enjoying the exercises and activities suggested in our handbook. I am sure you will find delight in becoming a group of people who write poetry.

From Dianna

This has been an incredible journey, learning to be unafraid to look deep into my emotional self and to be willing to put these thoughts into print, for others to see and to know.

"I have learnt to be strong and brave,
To dance in the light of my feelings,
And dance in the shadows they cast.
To weave tiny magical stories
With word threads that come from the heart."

My suggestion to you as a novice poet is to write your poetry for yourself. It's a wonderful way to get to know yourself better or your poetry pals and others reading your poetry. It's a way for them to connect more deeply with your insights and perhaps even themselves!

Creating poetry as a group has been a wonderful experience, challenging at times, with so many different ideas to consider, but always enriching in a literary way and so rewarding as a social opportunity to share and enjoy.

Happy poetry writing!

From Sue

I have always wanted to write and to be a writer. As women, we dedicate much of our lives to family, relationships, children, caring for parents or others and working. This inevitably gets in the way of creative pursuits such as writing or painting. Over the years, I have written many things but the ones that have been published have usually been through my employment. These have included resources for drama teaching in schools, papers about drama process or organisational change and development. At times of crisis in my life, I would find myself writing poetry, and when I had grandchildren, I wrote stories for them that I tried to illustrate!

It has been exhilarating in my retirement to develop a relationship with three other wonderful women who have allowed me to put aside my anxiety and inertia and once again enjoy playing around with words and poetic forms and rhythm and rhyme. When we started out writing poetry together, we barely knew each other. Now we have shared our highs and lows, explored our similarities and differences and laughed and cried together. I hope you too can experience the wonderful world of poetry with girlfriends.

Topic: Just for Enjoyment and Inspiration

Sometimes reading the works of others who are ordinary people just like you and me, provides welcome enjoyment and even inspiration that enhances our lives.

We hope that browsing through our poems gives you a platform to dive into your own poetry.

The Moon

The moon hung low over the highway tonight
Slipping behind overpasses, walkways, hills and trees
As I drifted down the freeway.

Orange balloon, enormous,
Stretched out at the sides, floating among the highway lights
Sometimes hanging lantern like,
Sometimes dropping suddenly
To blaze among the trees.

My mind slips free, I yearn to follow it
Above the shutdowns, anti-vaxers,
Deniers of climate change, politicians
And the just plain ignorant.

Orange morphs to lemon,
Softer, rounder, caught on the tip of the crane,
Then gone.
And will I see it as I creep towards death
Or will it pale under the clouds of gas, of dust,
Of colonists desperate to own it too?

I would slip into the basket of the shimmery globe
Drift away, settle on the highest hill,
And meditate on the foolishness of humans.
Would they listen? Or would I lie back on the grass and drink on
Watching the moon rise as the sun set
As I crawl into my last dark chrysalis.

—Sue Elmes

Nits Don't Like Hairspray

We all had a note when we came home from school
The three of us said . . . "It was the rule!"
"Nits," Mum screamed as though we had died
And rang Dad saying loudly . . . "I'm mortified!"

With only one car in the early days
Dad took it to work, and they shopped Saturdays.
"Pick up a nit comb on your way home
And don't stop at the pub," she said with a tone.

She grabbed the comb, no hello or a kiss
Olive oil at the ready she was in a right tizz.
They're in our ears we all started screamin'
She was ready for war with those little white vermin.

"Line up," she said and began to toil
Our hair now plastered with wretched olive oil.
She combed and combed dragging little blighters out,
"Got ya!" she yelled as we squirmed about.

This went on nightly for almost a week
And our friends made a comment that we started to reek.
It runs through the family the note had said
So she got Dad to check her neatly coiffed head.

She was proud of her hair worn in a beehive bun,
Never a hair out of place even on the run.
"Did YOU get the crawlies friends enquired over a drink
No, nits don't like hair spray," she said with a wink.

—Kate Kennedy

Checkmate

Candle flickers
In the darkness of the night
Chess board set up
The kings never fight

Knights take up battle
Two up and one over
You teach her chess
But your war's never over

King on his colour
Backed up by his knight
Golden Eagles slay Rising Suns
Men die as they fight

She can't wear your medals
You tossed them away
No glory in battle
Checkmate every day

—Dianna Fames

The Pink Tree

The balcony is big they say
Too big for one they leave unsaid,
But there is wondering in their gaze
These are different days I think.

As the family gathers round
The balcony seems to shrink;
Then they go, and it's too big for one
I later think.

It doesn't seem right to call it home
Not yet, maybe never;
The balcony is big they say
Too big for one.

I look across the piles of soil
Where further building will commence,
And what I see is a pink tree in the distance
These are different days I think.

I see six years has hurried by.
The balcony is big they say,
But now there is puzzle in their glance,
Too many plants, they roll their eyes.

Happy gatherings have come and gone,
And room for one more table on
That too big balcony, too big for one;
But it's okay when all's said and done.

Just right for the wheelchair now
That my beloved lives next door.
He rolls his eyes too at plant greenery
When his wheel catches on the jade.

The further building is here right now
Close to the big balcony.
The tree I love I cannot see
But I know you are there for me.

—Jude Comerford

Topic: Just for Enjoyment and Inspiration

Mass Graves . . . Lament for Little Ones Lost

I find I have no faith
no will to make that leap
to God, to heaven or a flaming hell.

But, once more
they found mass graves;
not in Serbia, the Congo, the hills of Mexico
or the Covid ravaged cemeteries of Europe
and America.

Three hundred tiny bodies lay buried
in the shadow of the trees and walls,
Discarded, dumped, abandoned by the orphanage.
Tossed into the green lushness of the world outside their walls.

And did the Priests, the Brothers,
the Nuns and Holy Sisters, the nurses and the carers
even take a moment?
To think, to pray, to beg
their God's indulgence for these sinful ones,
born outside the Church's holy rules?

And when they died, these holy folk
smug in their righteous ignorance,
did they decay in peace into the soil,
their nutrients melting to feed the worms and microbes
of this unholy site? This Irish burial ground.

And did their God smile kindly on their pious hands,
Or did His Son smite them for all time?
Condemned to cycle through their karma,

like these abandoned babes, ripped from their mothers,
and their grandmothers; unloved, unfed,
clothed in rags, and not the Bishop's velvet cloth?

I find I have no faith
no will to make that leap
to God, to heaven or a flaming hell.

But if my belief, my faith, would lead those priests,
those holy sinners to their rightful punishment, and
the little ones could rest in the paradise
of loving arms through all eternity;
I might, perhaps, have cause to reconsider.

—Sue Elmes

Topic: Just for Enjoyment and Inspiration

Treasure Trove

A birthday picnic, eleven years old, bus hired for the day.
Wattle! We plucked off boughs, laughing, so gay
The colour, the smell, the feel, the fun
A wonderful garden, of fear there was none.

We carried our gold to the bus and stored it,
Layer upon layer on the back seat, up lit
By the glow of our treasure, how happy, we basked,
Discoverers were we, yet we hadn't even asked.

Man, in uniform stepped onto the bus,
Saw our wattle and made such a fuss.
"This is a National Park," he told us,
Then threw our beautiful boughs on the boulders.

"But they are just for our mothers," we said.
The man in the uniform shook his head.
"You two try to do this once more
And, believe me, you'll just get what for!"

Yet he still threw our boughs on the bounders that day
We pleaded, there was nothing more we could say.
Still there was so much joy in our doing,
No sense in keeping our anger brewing.

Memory is funny in its own way,
Why do I think of that day today?
Decades and decades of life have passed,
But we still love our wattle to the very last.

—JUDE COMERFORD

Covid—I'll Choose

So you're anti-vax, and you don't give toss,
Who you infect, or cause a great loss.
What are you thinking, you don't seem to care,
You wander all over, a cough here and there.

With your banners and placards, "It's my right to choose,"
Did you ever think what your actions might lose,
A child, a mother, a dad, or a brother,
A grandchild, a friend or a special other?

What's your excuse, go on please do tell,
'Cos nothing I could think of, could possibly sell.
With three million dead, words of love left unsaid,
Your excuse leaves the world . . . exposed . . . full of dread.

So you'll rely on the herd, no thought what you'd bring
To the millions of people, who'll do the right thing.
The lucky country, of that there's no doubt,
Consider the countries, which are going without.

Fellow Australians should it be up to me,
You must choose an island way out to sea,
With like-minded people arriving every day,
You'd risk it all to get your own way.

Have your right to choose and do as you please,
We can now live our lives feeling safe and at ease.

—Kate Kennedy

Waking Up

Kookaburras chortle a monkey like yodel,
Time for the sun to rise.
Other birds follow, whoops and whistles
And whip cracking sounds.
Cockatoos screech and squark
A raucous din of repetition.
Too early for me to rise, yet
Can't get back to the safety of slumber.

Morning, the biggest challenge,
Most difficult of all.
Physical unsteadiness,
A cloud of mental haze,
Senses jumbled, distorted.
Am I still in the dream state?
What was that noise?
Is it a snake or a sock on the floor?

Misjudging shapes and distances,
Colliding with door knobs and frames,
Bruises on hips and thighs.
Teetering at the top of the stairs
A cup in each hand,
Left over tea from the night before,
And unfinished water.
This is the start to my day.

—Dianna Fames

Yoga Nature

Here you are, there you are
You have always been there.
I've known you for a decade,
But you are a thousand decades on.

You are impermanent Nature.
Every Thursday we gather on your site.
We breathe, we feel, we listen,
We breathe in, we breathe out.

We become one with the landscape,
We become one with the valley.
Present in the moment,
Time, coming, pausing, passing.

Nowhere else to be,
Nothing else to do.
Trees are greener here.
Birds sing sweeter here.

The breeze is softer here.
We breathe in, we breathe out.
We find peace.
At one with Yoga Nature.

—Dianna Fames

Topic: Just for Enjoyment and Inspiration

Breakdown

My being shifts, changes, now tangible,
Made up of proteins, solid, a woman of substance;
But as I float upon the water
The image of Lot's Wife fixes in my brain.

Was she a woman of substance?
A wife, a mother, she sang in the squares of Sodom,
fed her family, washed their clothes, wiped their fevered brows.
But as she left her city, watching for her daughters,
Trembling at the loss her heart now held,

She turned, and turning her heart, her body,
A solid, tangible presence, real physical matter, now
Coalesced into a block of salt,
Sodium chloride, a block, a rock;
Substare[3], substant, substantia
Her essence standing firm.

Salt! A substance, a uniform and definite composition
But the undertow pulls me down,
Whirlpooling me, watery hands clasping shoving!
Am I protected if I don't look back?

My swimmers gone, my goggles lost, hair loose.
Blindly I dissolve into the water
Liquid now, no substance now
No permanent composition, I drift
Lost undecided I no longer know myself.
No influence no power to gather up the crystals
And conjure back my substance.

—Sue Elmes

---

[3] Substare: Latin, to stand firm

The Transformation

When does a woman leave the girl behind?
That elusive transformation . . . it makes you think.
Growing up I was always the girl next door.
Maybe the beginning of my cycle, drew it near.

At fifteen I'm the girl in the local chemist
All grown up on the outside, not a woman then!
My twenty first birthday, a milestone for sure
"Hey girl," someone said, "You're now legal to drink."

Would it be when I married at twenty-two?
"Do you take this woman . . ." the word was said
But who cares what it meant as my new husband said
"You're my girl forever, now that we're wed."

"Take baby to his mother," the ward sister ordered
At twenty-four, insecure, how will I cope?
The divorce lawyer asked was I absolutely sure;
A woman would know but I'm lost and torn.

"Thanks lady," said the busker when I threw him the coin
At thirty-five, still no confidence, definitely not then
But at forty I remarry . . . new hope for the future
"Do you take this woman," I might be getting there!

Get up kid and let the woman sit down
Seated comfortably, aged fifty, I ponder again.
Now at sixty-nine and a grandmother of three
Surely I'm a woman, the transformation complete.

But if it ever happened I really don't know
'Cos sometimes I'm the girl from so long ago.

—KATE KENNEDY

Eradication

They are burning bamboo in the valley
White smoke rising up to the sky
Black Wedgetails glide on the thermals
It's been decided the bamboo must die.

Men on the ground chainsaw and flame it
That's what they are trained to do
All uniformed up in retardant gear
They have no memory of you.

I gaze up at the eagles
Is that you, Faye?
I breathe in the smoke, is that you?
Are you saddened by what they do?

Is this just the way it has to be?
Your life in the valley now past
I struggle with this, while men slash and burn
I want everything to last.

I wave at the eagles, they see me
They're Spirit Guardians in the sky
They circle me with their blessings
One day they will teach me to fly.

—Dianna Fames

Captured

My feet emerge from the bed and
My body follows. Silently I slip across the room
The bathroom swallows me.
I have no purpose, I am in stasis,
Isolation has captured me. One of six
I wait to see which skittle falls next.

I will be calm I tell my mind.
I read, cook and meditate.
I make an Isolation apple pie,
I paint more spikes on the prickly cactus
And I turn to my book.

This book explores the spaces
The Places between worlds, where the losers lurk,
The has-beens and the dispossessed fall
Into the cracks and land in London Below [4].

---

[4] London Below is a term used by Neil Gaiman in his urban fantasy series "Neverwhere." In this series, London Below is a magical realm that coexists with the more familiar London, referred to as London Above. There are other books also known as urban fantasy that are based on the myths and legends of big cities, such as London. For example, "The Rivers of London" series by Ben Aaronovich.

Topic: Just for Enjoyment and Inspiration

The news haunts me,
I watch the floods and war in Europe
Reality and fiction collide
The horrors of the dark,
The nightmare games and monsters
Merge from page to screen and back to haunt my dreams.

There is no escape, no peace
Yet I sit safely in my son's home
A prisoner, an isolate, waiting for the end to come.

—SUE ELMES

Talking Teacups

During the Second World War,
When I was eight years old,
Every second Wednesday
My mother's lady friends
Came to play their game of cards.

I rushed home, dropped my schoolbag,
Hurried in to lean at the lounge room door.
Twisting my plaits, I waited to hear one lady, Eva.
I knew afternoon tea was over,
Now Eva would read the tea leaves in the empty cups.

Eva was special.
Young, fragile, titian hair swept into rolls
On either side of a centre part.
This made a kind of halo of a saintly sort.
Her heart-shaped face glowed with serenity,
In the reflection of Golden Cassia blooms outside the leadlight window.

Her slim hands were as fine
As the pale-yellow bone chinacup she held;
She looked into it, turning it this way and that.
Her eyes and her soft voice held a message.
"Ruby, things will get better for you. You will hear from your boy soon."
He was missing somewhere in the Pacific.

Eva gently handed the cup back.
Almost with reverence she took another one.
"Celia, I think you will meet

One of those American soldiers who are in town.
You will like him and he'll ask you to go back to the States."

Celia smiled but shook her head. Her husband had been killed
In earlier days of the war in Europe.
Then Eva spoke once more, now holding another cup.
"Sheila, don't worry, we'll see that you have
Enough ration coupons for your daughter's wedding breakfast."

The other women nodded knowingly,
They exchanged glances and smiled
As they gently rocked back and forth in their bridge chairs.
Mum signalled for me
To change out of my school clothes.

I happily wandered to my room,
Then the kitchen.
Mum had kept cake for me,
Cream-filled sponge cake with orange icing.
I ate it slowly as though in a dream.

I had such a warm feeling of well-being.
Not from the cake.
In my eight-year-old mind,
No matter what happened, while ever Eva could look
Into Mum's teacups, tell what she saw there,
Everything was going to be alright with the world.

—Jude Comerford

Going Home in the Fifties

The brakes of the tram screech to a halt;
The end of a long, wet work day for me.
I step down onto the road
My foot slipping on the running board.

A jab of pain but it's fine.
I fix my shoulder bag in place
And make it to the footpath
Sloshing in pools of rainwater.

"Paper, paper" rings out from the boy
Selling the evening newspapers;
"Read all about it!
The latest from the Korean War."

Just sixteen, but this news about that War
Has been reaching me for years.
I pass the paper boy by, cross the busy road
To jetty number five.

Air steamy, carbon monoxide pungent,
Accelerators rev, tyres slick on the sodden road.
Car horns compete. I bump shoulders
With other people who jostle hard,
Before I reach my ferry jetty.

Then to the "Paper Shop" on the jetty,
A magnet for commuters.
Buffeted by the crows, I am one of them.
Treat myself to a magazine, it's Friday night.

The continuous clink, clink, clink
Of threepences, sixpences, shillings and half-crowns
Going in and out of the cash register.
The smell of all kinds of exotic, crisp new scents reach me.
It conjures up unknown, foreign places, other times.

Pay for my "Women's Weekly" with a shilling,
Receive my threepence change.
My gloved hand runs over the cover,
I imagine I can feel its exciting gloss.

Soon on the ferry gliding past Bennelong Point,
where one day an Opera House will stand.
Now it is still a tram depot.
Further across the water is the famous Harbour Bridge,
It is barely twenty years old. I thought it had been there forever.
At sixteen I had a lot of growing up to do.

—JUDE COMERFORD

Rescue

The day had started so badly,
So troubled was I in my mind,
Mistakes kept happening and sadly
No remedy could I find.

Then suddenly came the answer
And all was put right in the end;
I talked and then you listened
Because you are my caring friend.

—Jude Comerford

About the Authors

Jude Comerford

I grew up in Sydney and always loved living there. The joy of going "in to town" for the day and travelling across the harbour by ferry to work, stays with me even now that I am in my eighties.

I married at twenty-one, having met my husband on a driving holiday with my mother in country Queensland. While living and raising children there, the only way for me to keep in touch was by letters exchanged with family and friends.

I always loved to write, starting as a young child. When we moved to Brisbane twenty-five years later, I joined U3A. I had stories published in a U3A Redlands anthology and in a Society of Women Writers Queensland (SWWQ) anthology. I received two third-prize places in SWWQ Short Story competitions. I also co-authored a published novel, *The Written Word*, with a Redlands group of writers.

Having always written in short-story form, I was intrigued by the opportunity to explore poetry writing. I met a group of women at a writing course who introduced me to the poetic form. By stripping out all the connecting words in my stories, I could write poems that captured my thoughts and feelings.

Sue Elmes

My childhood was simple, idyllic and loving. I went off to University quite naïve and having no idea where I was headed. Looking back from my seventies, I am amazed at the things I have achieved and the experiences I have survived.

Married at eighteen, we managed to raise a child and finish our studies. I headed off to be a teacher of English, History and Drama, having more children along the way. I changed employment at least four times, survived cancer, tried to live by my feminist ideals, watched our children grow up, find successful futures and have children themselves.

In every role I took—work, community, professional associations and performances—writing was a significant element. I love words and using them clearly and simply, constructing a product that can explain, clarify, bring joy and sorrow and allow the reader to experience a range of points of view.

In times of stress and anxiety, or when my depression is at its worst, I find myself turning to poetry. Reading it, writing it, meditating on it, reminds me I am not alone in my experiences. Now, in retirement, I travel when money and health allows. I have discovered watercolour painting, and I love to write by myself and with friends. Leading a group of older women and men who write and edit their own poems also brings me great joy.

Dianna Fames

It has been and continues to be a life that involves being part of nature. Beginning as a child from Aotearoa who played on the gorse-covered foothills of the capital's Tararua mountains and learnt to climb apple trees that bore fruit, both sweet and sour. Then as an adolescent who learnt to swim in the muddy waters of Onerahi Bay, a magical place framed by giant Pohutukawa trees.

With young adulthood came a one-way ticket to the much older sister-land of Terra Australis with family in tow. It was here that an even brighter sun shone upon a seemingly endless, easterly coastline. From the Border Ranges all the way to the warm, tropical rainforests of Far North Queensland, what grandeur, what spaciousness, such an abundance of life's energy, food, shelter, community and purpose. Those industrious adult years spent tempering the urge to strive with an awareness of nature's gentle presence, being consoled and soothed and by her cool breezes, summer rains, seasonal changes, colours and patterns, sounds and silence.

Now, as a senior adult, beginning to understand the journey taken as well as the path that has been followed. Always guided by a sense of nature combined with a consciousness of nature's principles. This insight continues to unfold here in the nurturing dry rainforest and eucalypt forest of South East Queensland, once inhabited by the Jagera and Turrbal people. It is a place where one is never alone, a place where one is always surrounded by the abundant energy of life. A place to write, a place to be.

Kate Kennedy

The end of WWII was a tumultuous and unsettling time for those who had served. One of these people was my Polish father who had met and married my mother while stationed in Scotland. Going forward a couple of years, at the age of two, I found myself emigrating with my parents, in a very large ship, bound for Australia.

Growing up in a suburb of Brisbane, the hot sunny days were spent playing with the neighbourhood kids, riding bikes, building cubbies and exploring the bush up the back. All this and gaining citizenship made us Aussies through and through.

Motherhood and a career spent travelling around Australia writing and delivering leadership and personal development programs inspired me and my writing. These experiences, combined with a passion for travelling, have taken me to many interesting and unique parts of the world. Retirement was a shock and writing was one activity that gave me meaning and purpose.

I can tell a good story, but writing one was challenging. Joining a local writer's group, I had some short stories published. Recently, I decided to venture into the world of poetry. I discovered that short stories can be turned into amazing poetry. The trick was to be word economical while not losing meaning and sentiment. In doing so, I found a freedom of expression and enjoyed exploring and searching for exactly the right word.

Bibliography

Here are some books you might find helpful.
1. Dictionaries and Thesaurus
2. Internet
   - In the 21st century, the internet is a fabulous tool for anyone wanting information. We went to it for definitions, rhyming words, grammar, synonyms, spelling, information about poets, their views and individual style.
3. *Ode Less Travelled: A Guide to Writing Poetry*. Stephen Fry. London: Penguin Random House UK, 2005.
4. *A Poetry Handbook: A Prose Guide to Understanding and Writing Poetry*. Mary Oliver. New York: Mariner, 1994.
5. *Elizabeth Bishop – A Miracle for Breakfast*. Megal Marshall. Boston, MA, United States: Houghton Miffun, 2017
6. *Shakespeare on Toast: Getting a Taste for the Bard*. Ben Crystal. London, UK: Icon Books Ltd, 2008.

www.ingramcontent.com/pod-product-compliance
Lightning Source LLC
Chambersburg PA
CBHW052149110526
44591CB00012B/1912